INDIANA STATE POLICE:
AGE DISCRIMINATION

INDIANA STATE POLICE:
AGE DISCRIMINATION

Davis, Ph.D and Allen, MPA

To order additional copies of this book, contact:
Xlibris
1-888-795-4274
www.Xlibris.com
Orders@Xlibris.com
730866

Preface

This book may prove valuable to anyone who is interested in joining the Indiana State Police but who is currently over the department's maximum age limit for initial hire or rehire. This book contains information that may prove valuable to anyone who may decide to challenge the department's maximum age-hiring policy in court. The Indiana State Police's maximum age limit policy violates both state and federal laws. However, they are currently able to enforce their age limit policy because they have historically controlled incriminating information, which they do not want to advertise. A recent U.S. 7th Circuit Court ruling has shifted the burden of proof from the complainant to the Indiana State Police, requiring them to produce incriminating information, if challenged in court. This book provides information that may be used to overcome the barriers put in place by the Indiana State Police.

Authors

Wayne L. Davis, Ph.D.

Wayne L. Davis holds the following degrees: a Bachelor of Science in Electrical Engineering, a Master of Science in Business Administration, and a Ph.D. in Criminal Justice. Dr. Davis has graduated from city, state, and federal law enforcement academies and has over 20 years of law enforcement experience with city, state, and federal law enforcement agencies. Dr. Davis was a field training officer with the Indiana State Police. In addition, Dr. Davis has received the U.S. Customs & Border Protection Scholastic Award and the U.S. Customs & Border Protection Commissioner's Award.

Christopher Allen, MPA

Christopher Allen holds the following degrees: an Associate in Criminal Justice from Central Arizona College, a Bachelor in Criminal Justice from Ball State University, and a Master of Public Affairs from Indiana University. In addition, he has over 20 years of law enforcement experience with the Indiana State Police and with the Arizona, Indiana, and Florida Department of Corrections, respectively.

Davis   Allen

Table of Contents

List of Tables

List of Figures

CHAPTER 1

INDIANA STATE POLICE: AGE DISCRIMINATION

Historically, the consensus theory, which is based on the assumption that laws represent the views of the greatest normative consensus, has played a major role in understanding law and human behavior (Akers & Sellers, 2009). During the 1960s, however, the conflict theory, which is based on the assumption that competing groups struggle for power, became the forefront of criminological theory. According to the conflict theory, the public disagrees on many social issues, which are usually due to differentials in wealth and power (Barkan, 2006). The most powerful groups gain control of the government and they adopt their values as the legal standards of behaviors. Instead of serving the public, those individuals in power pass laws and policies to protect their own self-interests (Vold et al., 2002). Consequently, the people with power are able to pursue their self-interests while the people with less power, usually minorities, are unable to pursue their self-interests because their actions are defined as criminal.

According to the Declaration of Independence, the U.S. government derives its power from the individuals that it governs (Hames & Ekern, 2005). Indeed, because there are more than 400 U.S. residents for every full-time sworn police officer, law enforcement requires that people voluntarily comply with the law and assist with law enforcement efforts (Federal Bureau of Investigation, 2011). Thus, it seems clear that the police need to earn the public's trust.

When a police department demonstrates that it will engage in less than ethical behaviors during court proceedings in order to discriminate against a protected class, that department may lose its credibility and the public's support. However, unlike federal law enforcement agencies, local law enforcement agencies do not enforce the Giglio policy. In U.S. law, Giglio information refers to material tending to impeach the character or testimony of the prosecution witness in a criminal trial (U.S. Department of Homeland Security, 2004). Giglio mandates that the prosecution disclose any and all information that may be used to impeach the credibility of the law enforcement officers. Impeachment information under Giglio includes acts of misconduct, such as perjury during civil cases. Once federal officers are caught lying, their deceitful nature can be introduced in future criminal trials. As a result, such federal officers become useless in court and will be fired by their departments.

Local law enforcement departments, like the Indiana State Police, do not enforce the Giglio policy. Thus, local police officers may not be discouraged from committing perjury. In addition, police officers are often immune from libel and slander lawsuits if committed during their official duties (669.14 Exceptions, n.d.). In Iowa, for example, state law clearly indicates that the state police have civil immunity from "any claim arising out of assault, battery, false imprisonment, false arrest, malicious prosecution, abuse of process, libel, slander, misrepresentation, deceit, or interference with contract rights" (669.14 Exceptions, number 4). Because libel and slander violations are not considered constitutional violations, victims may have little recourse in such situations. In other words, a libel victim may not be able to sue the officer in state or federal court (Freedman, 2009). It is a public disservice when police officers abuse those whom they have sworn to protect and serve. It should be no surprise to the police that many residents are fed up and are reacting via protests and violence.

Indiana State Police: Age Discrimination & Violation of Law

The following information may prove valuable to anyone who is interested in joining the Indiana State Police but who is currently over the department's maximum age for initial hire or rehire. Although the maximum age limit is currently 39 years of age, it used to be 34 years of age. Below is information that may prove valuable to anyone who may decide to challenge the department's age-hiring policy in court. **It only takes one person who has the resources and who is interested in challenging the Indiana State Police's maximum age limit policy to change state police practice.**

Table 1

Age Discrimination Case Synopsis (Davis v. Indiana State Police, 2008; Davis v. Whitesell, 2011).

Point	Chronological Actions
1	1996 - The Indiana State Police (ISP) fired Christopher ALLEN at the Indiana State Police Academy because ALLEN had a benign brain tumor.
2	Christopher ALLEN hired a lawyer and started a lawsuit against the ISP.
3	The ISP provided medical records that ALLEN was unfit for duty.
4	ALLEN never saw ISP doctors for the brain tumor and claimed that the medical records were false.
5	ISP then claimed to have destroyed/lost ALLEN's personnel records, including the false medical records.

6	1998- Because of the ISP's unethical behaviors, ALLEN was confident that he would win a lawsuit. As part of a legal settlement, the ISP decided to rehire ALLEN. The ISP rushed to rehire ALLEN before he was over the maximum age limit and the ISP had a special ceremony to appoint ALLEN as a trooper (he was the only one appointed that day). Several command personnel, a judge, and the media were present. However, ALLEN was now over the department's maximum age limit for new hirees. This is clear evidence that ALLEN did not slip through the cracks as the ISP would later argue in the DAVIS case.
7	2005 – DAVIS left the ISP to join U.S. Dept. of Homeland Security.
8	2006 – DAVIS sought rehire with the ISP. DAVIS proceeded through the rehire process and was welcomed back as a trooper by the Superintendent and Board.
9	Shortly thereafter, the ISP claimed that DAVIS was too old to be rehired and that there was something in his background. DAVIS was denied rehire.
10	DAVIS inquired about the "something in the background" but the ISP did not respond.
11	DAVIS considered whether to file an age discrimination lawsuit in state or federal court. State Court – maximum age for new employees violates state law (Indiana Code 10-11-2-10). The Indiana law states that the Superintendent shall set standards of qualifications in conformity with the plans and standards most widely adopted in other states, dominions, and provinces. However, only about a dozen state police agencies have a maximum age limit for new employees. Federal Court – maximum age for new employees violates federal law (Age Discrimination in Employment Act, 29 U.S.C. §§621-33a)

12	DAVIS filed an age discrimination lawsuit against the ISP in federal court. Davis sought a court system not affiliated with the State of Indiana to evaluate the case.
13	2008 - U.S. 7th Circuit Court stated that wherever the law draws a line there will be cases on either side of the line that will be functionally indistinguishable; however, that does not invalidate the line. If the ISP had violated its age limit policy in the past, then the department's age policy cannot be enforced. In addition, the Court ruled that instead of the plaintiff proving that the department has violated the age policy, the police department must now show that it has not violated the policy (i.e., the burden of proof has shifted to the police department, who has control over the records). However, the U.S. 7th Circuit Court also ruled that under federal law, a bona fide policy may be senseless and may violate state law (in other words, statutory law cannot be conflated to constitutional criteria).
14	DAVIS subpoenaed his personnel records, all electronic records related to the case, and the hiring records of the ISP to determine the age of all candidates newly hired. The ISP claimed to have destroyed/lost select information from DAVIS' personnel file and all electronic records related to the case.
15	The ISP only provided partial information on its past hiring practices. The ISP only provided about half of the information subpoenaed. DAVIS requested that all of the information be provided but the ISP refused to provide all of the subpoenaed information. The U.S. District Court did not force the ISP to turn over its records.

16   ISP officers were deposed about the "something in the background". Their arguments were that Davis failed to disobey the district commander, Davis failed to use force against an unarmed female who had not violated the law, and Davis, who worked the midnight shift, was rarely seen during the day shift. In addition, the troopers claimed to have been unable to remember fundamental details when they were deposed. This was important because the officers were interviewed by the Department of Homeland Security about Davis just prior to the court proceedings and now their stories had changed. By conveniently forgetting important facts about their past actions and what they had said, and having no written documentation to support their accusations, they did not have to clarify or expand on any information that may have been detrimental to their case. They simply stated something like, *I have no records and no memories of the case, but if I said it, it must be true. I stand by initial decision, no matter what.* For example, an administrative officer was deposed and he claimed that one of the troopers being deposed had interviewed him and had changed the meaning of his statement to mean something completely different in order to make DAVIS look bad. When the officer was presented with that information, he stated that once his mind is made up, nothing will change it. This indicates that the officer does not care about the facts, that the officer has a personal agenda, and the officer will attempt to win at any cost. **This is dangerous for the general public.** Indiana State Police lawyers argued that it does not matter what the officers stated, as long as the Superintendent believed them to be true (good faith). Subsequently, when put on the spot, the Superintendent dropped the "something in the background" and claimed that age was the sole factor for failing to rehire DAVIS.

17	The Indiana State Police contacted ALLEN and attempted to secure a second identification for him, which indicated that he was not over the maximum age limit when rehired. ALLEN refused to cooperate. The Indiana State Police failed to obtain the second identification. Subsequently, the Indiana State Police admitted to the U.S. 7th Circuit Court that the department had hired ALLEN when he was over the maximum age limit. However, the department claimed that it was a clerical mistake. The ISP stated that they hired thousands of employees and that ALLEN simply slipped through the cracks (the Indiana State Police only supplied about 1,170 records when they were subpoenaed, which is an admission that they failed to honor the subpoena).
18	2011- The U.S. 7th Circuit Court ruled for the Indiana State Police. The Indiana State Police argued that their hiring of ALLEN was a solitary failure to enforce their age limit policy and was the result of a clerical error rather than discretion to disregard the written requirements. Because DAVIS did not take issue with this characterization, there was no material dispute requiring a trial. **The circumstances about ALLEN's special appointment became available to DAVIS after the ruling.** The U.S. 7th Circuit Court did not say that DAVIS was wrong, only that he had failed to prove his case.

"I Do Not Remember"

When Indiana State Police officers were deposed and caught in less than competent/truthful situations, they simply responded that they did not remember how they made their decisions and that they had no documentation to refresh their memories. In other words, saying *"I do not remember"* is a technique used by police officers to escape bad situations. In this way, they can always remember select information later, when it is convenient, without contradiction. This will be hard for a plaintiff to overcome.

Figure 1. Indiana State Police reaction to subpoena

Indiana State Police Age Discrimination Case

During the Indiana State Police Academy in October 1996, Christopher ALLEN was told by his personal doctor in Carmel, Indiana that he had a benign brain tumor. His doctor stated that it could be removed and, once removed, ALLEN would be able to perform all police duties. ALLEN reported this fact to the Indiana State Police, who stated that it was no big deal. However, in November 1996, the Indiana State Police told ALLEN to quit or else he would be fired. ALLEN refused to quit, so he was fired.

ALLEN had surgery and had the brain tumor removed in January 1997. Soon afterward, ALLEN stated that the Indiana State Police had produced medical records from its affiliated doctor, who claimed that ALLEN was unfit for duty. ALLEN filed a lawsuit and challenged the medical records because ALLEN had never seen the department's affiliated doctor. In other words, the Indiana State

Police had produced false medical records. The Indiana State Police realized that they were in trouble when ALLEN's lawyer requested all of their records. Subsequently, the Indiana State Police claimed to have destroyed/lost ALLEN's personnel records, including the false medical records.

As a consequence of ALLEN's lawsuit, the Indiana State Police agreed to settle the case by having a special appointment to re-hire ALLEN. ALLEN was the only trooper that the Indiana State Police hired on that particular day, which was February 2, 1998. However, the Indiana State Police hired ALLEN after he had already passed the maximum age limit for rehire (which was 34 years of age at the time). In 2011, the Indiana State Police admitted to the U.S. 7th Circuit Court during the *Davis v. Indiana State Police/Whitesell* case that ALLEN was hired after he was over the maximum age limit. However, the Indiana State Police claimed that ALLEN was hired over the age limit because they hired thousands of employees and that ALLEN simply slipped through the cracks due to a clerical error. This is a false statement. Again, due to a legal settlement, ALLEN was a special appointment and he was the only trooper hired on February 2, 1998, which can be verified via Indiana State Police records.

In 2005, Wayne DAVIS left the Indiana State Police and joined the U.S. Department of Homeland Security. After about two months with the U.S. Department of Homeland Security, DAVIS wanted to return to the Indiana State Police. DAVIS re-applied to the Indiana State Police, passed all of the tests (e.g., polygraph, physical, psychological), and was welcomed back to the Indiana State Police by the Superintendent and the Board. Shortly thereafter, the Indiana State Police stated that DAVIS was over the maximum age limit for new hires and that he would not be rehired.

DAVIS challenged the department's maximum age limit policy in federal court (*Davis v. Indiana State Police*, 2008; *Davis v. Whitesell*, 2011). The U.S. District Court ruled against DAVIS. DAVIS appealed the case to the U.S. 7th Circuit Court. The U.S. 7th Circuit Court ruled that DAVIS had the right to collect Indiana State Police records to see if the department had made exceptions to its age hiring practice in the past. Thus, DAVIS subpoenaed all of the hiring records and electronic communications related to the case. DAVIS wanted to know the age of all Indiana state police officers at the time they were hired; DAVIS also wanted to know if the department engaged in less than ethical behaviors during his rehire process, which would be recorded in the electronic records. DAVIS suspected that the department's management ordered a detective to file a false report (related to the department's claim that there was something in DAVIS' background). The Indiana State Police resisted. The Indiana State Police claimed to have destroyed/lost many of DAVIS' personnel records and all of the electronic records related to the case. In addition, the Indiana State Police refused to turn over all of the subpoenaed documents that they did possess related to the age of new hirees. Several years later, the Indiana State Police still only produced about half of the subpoenaed hiring records. The Indiana State Police provided DAVIS with about 1,170 hiring records, but they clearly indicated to the U.S. 7th Circuit Court that there were thousands of hiring records when the department argued that ALLEN slipped through the cracks.

The limited records that the Indiana State Police did provide were cross-referenced against the Indiana State Police yearbooks; much of the information that was subpoenaed was missing. DAVIS' lawyer filed several motions with the U.S. District Court for the Indiana State Police to provide the rest of the information. The Indiana State Police refused to comply with the subpoena. Subsequently, the U.S. District Court ruled for the state. In the end, the U.S. District Court stated that DAVIS had failed to obtain enough information to prove his case. DAVIS again appealed to the U.S. 7th Circuit Court. In the end, DAVIS failed to get a jury trial and his case was dismissed because he had failed to obtain enough information to prove his case (he never did get all of the subpoenaed information) and he failed to argue that ALLEN was a special appointment. **The circumstances about ALLEN's special appointment became available to DAVIS after the ruling.** The U.S. 7th Circuit Court did not say that DAVIS was wrong, only that he had failed to prove his case. Had DAVIS argued the following points in the appropriate court, the results may have been different.

Table 2
Legal Issues not Addressed in the DAVIS Case that may be argued in a future Court Case

Item	Legal Issues **not** Addressed in the DAVIS Case	Appropriate Court
1	The Indiana State Police's hiring practice is not in compliance with Indiana state law (Indiana Code 10-11-2-10) (LexisNexis, 2008; Office of Code Division, n.d.). The Indiana law states that the Superintendent shall set standards of qualifications in conformity with the plans and standards most widely adopted in other states, dominions, and provinces. Only about a dozen states have maximum age limit policies for new hirees.	State
2	The Indiana State Police had a special appointment and hired Christopher ALLEN while he was over the ISP maximum age limit, which was 34 years of age at the time. He was the only one hired on February 2, 1998, which can be verified via Indiana State Police hiring records. This demonstrates that the hiring of ALLEN was not a clerical error (Indiana State Police argued that the department hired thousands of employees and that ALLEN slipped through the cracks).	Federal

3	At least two Superintendents since 1996 were hired over the maximum age limit. Superintendent Whitesell patrolled the highways as a state police officer. In order to comply with the law, a Superintendent can be hired from within the department. Indiana Code 10-11-2-6 does not excuse the Superintendent from meeting the age requirement ("Indiana Code", 2014).	State/Federal
4	The Indiana State Police's new hiree maximum age limit is not a constant. The Indiana State Police's maximum age limit for new employees changed from 34 to 39 years of age around the year 2005. The increase in age allowed certain individuals to be hired who were currently over the maximum age limit. The U.S. 7th Circuit Court ruled that a bona fide age policy cannot be spun for an occasion (Davis v. Indiana State Police, 2008).	Federal

Table 3

Questionable Behaviors of the Indiana State Police

Item	Unethical Behaviors of the Indiana State Police
1	The Indiana State Police threatened to fire ALLEN, who is black, if he did not quit due to a benign, correctable medical condition. ALLEN did not quit, so he was fired. White cadets who had medical conditions were not fired.
2	The Indiana State Police provided false medical records during ALLEN's case.
	The Indiana State Police destroyed ALLEN's personnel records during his lawsuit, including the false medical records.
3	The Indiana State Police claimed to have destroyed select information from DAVIS' personnel file during his lawsuit.

4	The Indiana State Police claimed to have destroyed/lost sought after electronic evidence related to DAVIS' case.
5	The Indiana State Police made accusations that DAVIS has something in his background to use as a backup plan in case they lost the age discrimination argument.
6	Several Indiana State Police officers were deposed. When caught in deception, the officers claimed that they did not remember fundamental details related to their claims and they did not have any notes or reports to refresh their memories. However, even though they could not remember past events, they continued to argue that their decisions were unquestionable.
7	The "something in the background" included the following: DAVIS did not use physical force against a female, who did nothing wrong (the trooper stated that DAVIS should have used forced because, as the trooper drove along the highway, he could see that the female was walking into a building away from DAVIS as DAVIS exited his vehicle, which is resisting); DAVIS, who worked the midnight shift, was rarely seen during the day shift; a probationary officer at the time stated that DAVIS refused to disobey the district commander; and a trooper stated that he talked with a lieutenant who knew DAVIS years earlier and the lieutenant stated that he would not rehire DAVIS. The lieutenant was subsequently deposed and he stated that the trooper's statement was false. When the trooper was presented with that information, he stated that once his mind is made up, nothing will change it. The trooper stated that the lieutenant's true meaning was irrelevant. This indicates that the trooper does not care about the facts, that the trooper has a personal agenda, and the trooper will attempt to win at any cost. **This is dangerous for the general public.**

8	Indiana State Police lawyers argued that it does not matter what the officers stated, as long as the Superintendent believed them to be true (good faith). When put on the spot, the Superintendent later claimed that age was the only reason DAVIS was not rehired.
9	The U.S. 7th Circuit Court allowed DAVIS to subpoena evidence. DAVIS subpoenaed evidence related to the case but the Indiana State Police refused to turn over all of the requested information. However, DAVIS noticed that ALLEN was over the maximum age limit when hired.
10	The Indiana State Police contacted ALLEN and attempted to secure a second identification for him, which indicated that he was not over the maximum age limit when rehired. ALLEN refused to cooperate. The Indiana State Police failed to obtain the second identification. Subsequently, the Indiana State Police admitted to the U.S. 7th Circuit Court that ALLEN was over the maximum age limit when rehired.
11	The Indiana State Police argued that hiring ALLEN over the maximum age limit was an honest mistake because they hired thousands of employees and he was an oversight. This is a false statement because the rehiring of ALLEN was part of a lawsuit settlement. There was a special appointment and ALLEN was the only trooper appointed on February 2, 1998, which can be confirmed by the ISP hiring records.
12	Soon after the final ruling in the *Davis v. Indiana State Police/Whitesell* case, the Indiana State Police initiated several internal investigations against Senior Trooper ALLEN. On or about July 11, 2011, ALLEN sent out a department-wide email message critiquing the department for current and past behaviors. Subsequently, ALLEN was suspended several times.

Table 4

Summary: Points of Interest in the DAVIS Case

Item	Points of Interest
1	Indiana State Police claimed to have destroyed/lost personnel records related to the case. In sum, there were about 25 different letters of recognition and commendation that had disappeared from DAVIS' file, which one Indiana State Police administrator stated was disturbing.
2	Indiana State Police claimed to have destroyed/lost all electronic records related to the case.
3	Indiana State Police failed to produce all hiring records.
4	Indiana State Police had a special appointment for Christopher ALLEN, who was over the maximum age limit for new hires.
5	Superintendents who were over the maximum age limit have been appointed to the ISP (the age limit can be satisfied if the Superintendent is appointed from within the department).
6	The ISP maximum age limit for new hires is illegal because it does not comply with the age policies of most other states (Indiana Code 10-11-2-10) (LexisNexis, 2008; Office of Code Division, n.d.).

Summary

The Indiana State Police has not always followed its age hiring policy. Indeed, the Indiana State Police had a special appointment as part of a lawsuit settlement and hired Christopher ALLEN, who they knew was over the maximum age limit for new hires. ALLEN was the only trooper that the department appointed on February 2, 1998 and he was over the maximum age limit. However, the Indiana State Police stated to the U.S. 7th Circuit Court that hiring ALLEN over the maximum age limit was a clerical mistake (*Davis v. Indiana*

State Police, 2011). The Indiana State Police Department had to say that because making an exception to its age hiring policy would have voided the policy. Although DAVIS failed to prove his case, this does not mean that DAVIS was wrong. **The information about ALLEN's special appointment became available to DAVIS after the U.S. 7th Circuit Court's ruling and it was not argued in the case.** Another person can follow up and challenge the Indiana State Police's maximum age hiring policy in either federal or state court.

When Indiana State Police officers were deposed and caught in less than competent/truthful situations, they simply responded that they did not remember how they made their decisions and that they had no documentation to refresh their memories. In other words, saying that they "do not remember" is a technique used by police officers to escape bad situations. In this way, they can always remember select information later, when it is convenient, without contradiction. This will be hard for a plaintiff to overcome.

In short, the poor person has little chance against a large police department. For example, it was a good defense strategy for the Indiana State Police to drag out the *DAVIS* case for almost 5 years, fighting to keep a jury from hearing the case. Individuals with limited financial resources may be forced to drop their cases against the department due to the high cost of legal fees (or the defendants may die or move away and lose interest). It would have been much faster and cost effective to let the *DAVIS* case go to a jury trial. However, the Indiana State Police did not want the case to go to a jury trial because they knew that the truth would come out. In other words, the only way the Indiana State Police could have won the case was to not let a jury hear the case. There was talk that if the department had lost the case, there might have been a significant cost to the department to restructure its pension program.

References

Age Discrimination in Employment Act (ADEA) (2016).
Retrieved from http://topics.hrhero.com/
age-discrimination-in-employment-act-adea/#

Akers, R.L., & Sellers, C. (2009). *Criminological theories:
Introduction, evaluation, and application* (5th ed.). New
York, NY: Oxford University Press.

Barkan, S. (2006). *Criminology: A sociological understanding* (3rd
ed.). Upper Saddle River, NJ: Pearson Prentice Hall.

Davis v. Indiana State Police, 541 F.3d 760 (7th Cir. September 3,
2008).

Davis v. Whitesell, No. 10-2617 (7th Cir. July 5, 2011).

Federal Bureau of Investigation (2011). *Crime in the United States,
2011*. Retrieved form https://www.fbi.gov/

Freedman, A. (2009, June 6). *Is the Pursuit of Happiness a Legal
Right?* Retrieved from http://www.quickanddirtytips.com/
business-career/legal/pursuit-happiness-legal-right

Hames, J., and Ekern, Y. (2005). *Constitutional law: Principles and
practice*. Clifton Park, NY: Thomson Delmar Learning.

Indiana Code - Section 10-11-2-6: Appointment of superintendent
(2014). Retrieved from http://codes.lp.findlaw.com/
incode/10/11/2/10-11-2-6

LexisNexis (2008). *Indiana criminal and traffic law manual*.
Charlottesville, VA: Matthew Bender.

Office of Code Division Indiana legislature Services Agency (n.d.).
    IC 10-11-2-10. Rank, grade, and position classifications.
    Retrieved from http://www.in.gov/legislative/ic/2010/title10/
    ar11/ch2.html

669.14 Exceptions. Retrieved from http://
    coolice.legis.iowa.gov/Cool-ICE/default.
    asp?category=billinfo&service=IowaCode&input=669#669.14

U.S. Department of Homeland Security (2004). *Law course for
    customs and border protection officers.* Longwood, FL:
    Gould.

Vold, G., Bernard, T., and Snipes, J. (2002). *Theoretical
    criminology* (5th ed.). New York, NY: Oxford University
    Press.

CHAPTER 2

CHRISTOPHER ALLEN: INDIANA STATE TROOPER

TO: Christopher Allen, Senior Trooper
           Toll Road, District 21

FROM: Paul Whitesell, Ph.D.
           Superintendent

SUBJECT: Disciplinary Action – Finding and Order

Senior Trooper Christopher Allen appeared before Lt. Colonel John W. Clawson, presiding as hearing officer, on August 23, 2011, at 10 A.M., for the purpose of answering to the charges preferred against him on August 16, 2011. Senior Trooper Allen admitted charge 1, and denied charges 2 and 3 that he violated Regulation 12, Sections 12-3(9), and 12-3(15), of the Personnel Rules of the Indiana State Police Department, to wit:

1. On or about July 11, 2011, Senior Trooper Allen did transmit an unauthorized message that disparages First Sergeant Tim Isenberg and the current Department administration with no legitimate Departmental business purpose, contrary to Indiana State Police Standard Operating Procedure CJD - 006, in violation of Regulation 12, Section 12-3(15).

2. On or about July 11, 2011, Senior Trooper Allen did negatively criticize the Department administration for requiring that Troopers perform the responsibilities of a Troopers such as: "whatever action is necessary to prevent and reduce crime, traffic crashes, and other disorder, using all of the imagination, initiative and ingenuity at their disposal, attempting to gain willful compliance with the law," contrary to Regulation 2, in violation of Regulation 12, Section 12-3(15).

3. On or about July 11, 2011, Senior Trooper Allen did convey false information to fellow officers or employees concerning official Department business when he made a statement in an e-mail to "ISP Everyone" to the effect that Colonel Weigand when the District Commander of the Redkey District filed a complaint against him with the Pendleton District Commander in 2003 for arresting drunk drivers in Redkey District, when, in fact, Lieutenant Lepper, Pendleton District Commander in 2003, received no such complaint from Colonel Weigand, in violation of Regulation 12, Section 12-3(9).

Senior Trooper Allen waived his right to an appearance before the Superintendent as provided by Indiana Code Section 10-11-2-15. After reviewing the evidence submitted to Lt. Colonel Clawson, and upon the recommendation of Lt. Colonel Clawson, it is my finding that the evidence does substantiate charges 1 and 3, but does not substantiate charge 2.

IT IS THEREFORE ORDERED:

1. That Senior Trooper Allen is suspended without pay for fifteen (15) days from the Department beginning September 12-16, September 19-23 and October 3-7, 2011.

2. That Lieutenant Kopinski or his designee pick up and hold the weapons, badges, all identification, Department computer and the assigned Commission of Senior Trooper Allen for the duration of the suspension.

3. That proper entries be made in payroll, personnel, and other records of the Department to carry out this order.

If you wish to appeal this disciplinary action, Section 15 of the Indiana State Police Act, codified at IC 10-11-2-15, prescribes the necessary procedure to follow to file an appeal with the Indiana State Police Board. An appeal must be made within fifteen (15) days of receipt of this order.

Paul Whitesell, Ph.D., Superintendent
Indiana State Police Department

Date: 8-30-2011

cc: Lt. Col. Parker
       Major Miller-Cronk
       Major Robbins
       Captain Coffee
       Lieutenant Kopinski
       Lieutenant Myers

Certified Mail No. 91 7190 0005 2720 0010 9122

On about July 11, 2011, Chris ALLEN wrote an opinion-based report that looked into the internal workings of the Indiana State Police. ALLEN described how the department has practiced age discrimination (by hiring him) and race/sex discrimination. ALLEN also claimed that the department has safety issues, quotas, low morale, and unfair disciplinary practices. Finally, ALLEN claimed that the department *dummied down* by dropping its educational requirement and has, perhaps, engaged in less than ethical behaviors. Although the department conducted an internal investigation, it remained silent on many of ALLEN's claims (Whitesell, 2011, August 30). Thus, this is an adoptive admission for many of the complaints (Klein, 1997). Below is some of the information related to ALLEN's department wide email message (Allen, 2011, July 11).

ALLEN's Internal Investigation

As a result of filing a complaint against the Indiana State Police, Senior Trooper ALLEN was investigated for various department violations and he was subsequently suspended (Whitesell, 2011, August 30). Senior Trooper ALLEN was charged with a) transmitting an unauthorized message on a department computer, b) negatively criticizing the department, and c) conveying false information by claiming that a formal complaint was filed against him, which involved arresting drunk drivers in a particular district. Although ALLEN was charged with three separate violations, the department did not find him guilty of criticizing the department. The following is a response to the Indiana State Police's findings.

Charge 1: Transmitting Unauthorized Information

ALLEN called the Indiana State Police (ISP) administrators the "Indiana Imbecile Club" (Allen, 2011, July 11, p. 7). Furthermore, ALLEN stated that the ISP lied to the U.S. 7th Circuit Court because the ISP knew that he was over the age limit when they hired him, that the ISP may have improperly taken federal monies, that the ISP is violating state law by having a maximum age limit (IC 10-11-2-10), that the ISP has dummied down the department, and that the ISP uses quotas to assess officer performance. Indeed, although ALLEN was found guilty of transmitting an unauthorized message, the ISP did not challenge the above claims on the *Finding and Order* of the internal investigation (Whitesell, 2011, August 30). Because the ISP failed to challenge the claims, they have made an adoptive admission to the claims. Indeed, Indiana State Police administrators are familiar with the law and the law states that when a party not does deny accusations made against him and the party had an opportunity to reply to the statements, that is an admission by silence (del Carmen, 2010; Klein, 1997; Whitesell, 2011, August 30).

Charge 2: Free Speech

Police officers have the Constitutional right of free speech (Peak, Gaines, & Glensor, 2010). Over the years, the courts and legislatures have bestowed or recognized a number of rights that police officers possess. Many of these rights are constitutionally guaranteed, but others have been adopted by legislative bodies or through union negotiations.

Although the right of freedom of speech is one of the most fundamental of all rights of Americans, the Supreme Court indicated in the *Pickering v. Board of Education* case that the State does have an interest in controlling the speech of its employees that differ significantly from the speech of the citizenry in general (Peak et al., 2010). Thus, the state may impose restrictions on its employees that it would not be able to impose on the citizenry at large. These restrictions must be reasonable, however.

A police regulation that is overly broad may be found to be an unreasonable infringement on a police officer's freedom of speech (Peak et al., 2010). **For example, there was a Chicago Police Department rule that prohibited any activity, conversation, or discussion that was derogatory toward the Department. That policy was found unreasonable by the Court.** The policy was unreasonable because such a rule prohibited all criticism of the agency by its officers, even in private conversation. Essentially, a department cannot arbitrarily regulate officers' speech. However, if officers make statements that adversely affect the department's operation, such as leaking information about an ongoing investigation, or making false statements, then the courts will generally rule in the State's favor to prohibit that kind of speech.

The Court ruling stated that police officers cannot provide false information or say something that interferes with law enforcement operations. Hence, ALLEN was not found guilty of negatively criticizing the department. In short, troopers charged with negatively criticizing their department in the future may want to challenge their police department's policy in court.

Charge 3: Conveying false information.

ALLEN stated he was told by a superior officer to stop arresting drunk drivers in a particular district (Allen, 2011, July 11). ALLEN stated that he wanted the order in writing, but the written order was not given. As a result of the situation, ALLEN stated that he suffered from stress and felt compelled to accept a transfer to a riverboat assignment, which was financially costly and emotionally draining. Even though the Indiana State Police did charge ALLEN for claiming that a formal complaint was filed against him by the superior officer, the Indiana State Police did not deny that ALLEN was orally ordered not to arrest drunk drivers in a particular district (Whitesell, 2011, August 30). The fact that the Indiana State Police did not deny these claims during the internal investigation is an adoptive admission that ALLEN was orally ordered not to arrest drunk drivers in a particular district (del Carmen, 2010; Klein, 1997; Whitesell, 2011, August 30). Lying requires intent. Thus, for disciplinary purposes, the ISP has equated non-verifiable information with deceit.

Whistle Blower: Indiana State Police Misconduct

Chris ALLEN was a veteran state trooper who claimed that the Indiana State Police department practices discrimination (Allen, 2011, July 11). He has challenged the Indiana State Police and, consequently, was suspended. However, during this situation, **the Indiana State Police did admit, via silence, that ALLEN's claims have substance** (Klein, 1997).

Age Discrimination

ALLEN stated that the Indiana State Police illegally practices age discrimination (Allen, 2011, July 11). Indiana Code 10-11-2-10 states that the Indiana hiring practice shall be consistent with most other states (LexisNexis, 2008). Only about a dozen state police agencies have age limits. Thus, Indiana State Police's age hiring policy of being less than 40 years of age is a violation of state law. This may be challenged in state court.

In addition, the Indiana State Police has not always followed their age hiring policy. Indeed, ALLEN stated that the Indiana State Police had a special appointment and hired him, who they knew was over the maximum age limit (Allen, 2011, July 11). He stated that he was the only trooper that the department appointed on February 2, 1998 and he was over the maximum age limit. The fact that the Indiana State Police did not deny these claims during ALLEN's internal investigation, which occurred after the DAVIS case, is an adoptive admission that they have violated their age hiring practice in the past (Klein, 1997; Whitesell, 2011, August 30).

Race Discrimination

Most Indiana police officers are male Caucasians (Long & Yerington, 2006). ALLEN, a black male trooper, stated that he had been targeted in the past because of his race (Allen, 2011, July 11). For example, ALLEN stated that he was fired during the Indiana

State Police academy because of a medical condition, which was correctable, even though Caucasian officers who had medical conditions were not fired. ALLEN was later rehired during a lawsuit.

While ALLEN was at the Indiana State Police academy, ALLEN was diagnosed with a benign brain tumor (Allen, 2011, July 11). After conferring with his doctor, ALLEN received a written letter that the condition, once corrected, would not affect his abilities to complete the academy. ALLEN stated that he informed the Indiana State Police of the situation but the Indiana State Police ordered him to resign. When ALLEN did not resign, he was fired.

Three Caucasian classmates, who had medical conditions, were also ordered to resign (Allen, 2011, July 11). However, when they failed to resign, they were not fired. ALLEN stated that race was a factor. The fact that the Indiana State Police did not deny these claims during ALLEN's internal investigation is an adoptive admission that they do practice race discrimination (Klein, 1997; Whitesell, 2011, August 30).

Quotas

Police departments do have quota systems (Miller, Schultz, & Hunt, 2011). Indeed, the Indiana State Police admitted that it has a quota system (Getts, 2011). Quota systems are used by police management to justify their own existence by providing information that uneducated individuals can easily understand (Kraska, 2004). Uneducated individuals may include police employees and local residents. In other words, it is very easy for a police department to show that the officers are doing work by advertising the number of tickets that the officers write. It requires more creativity to show police work if crime is prevented. Indeed, a study by Long and Yerington (2006) indicates that Indiana police administrators do not have a fundamental understanding of information that involves police work. This is supported by the fact that an Indiana trooper has referred to his administrators as the "Indiana Imbecile Club" (Allen, 2011, p.

7). Furthermore, because the Indiana State Police administrators did not dispute this claim during an internal investigation, this is, by definition, an adoptive admission (Klein, 1997).

If quotas are used to assess officer performance, then the objective of serving the public becomes less important (Kraska, 2004). For example, suppose there is no quota system in place and a trooper normally stops 5 cars per day and writes 5 citations. If a quota system is then implemented and requires the trooper to write 20 citations per day, the trooper may simply issue 20 citations to the occupants of the five cars. Instead of stopping more vehicles, the officers may simply provide vehicle occupants with more citations.

Quotas may have a negative effect on public perception and the overall morale of the officers. For example, a 10-year Indiana State police veteran recently quit the police department because he stated that the department has lost its focus on serving the public (Getts, 2011, July 10). The ex-trooper stated that the Indiana State Police micro-manages troopers and that the department uses quotas to judge police performance. The ex-trooper stated that the Indiana State Police overemphasizes traffic stops and fails to serve the public by undermining troopers' efforts to fight crime.

If Indiana State Police officers fail to write a certain number of tickets and warnings, then they are placed on probation (Allen, 2011, July 11). Consequently, troopers may be motivated to falsify their numbers in order to stay out of trouble. Moreover, there are many aspects of police work that are not measured by a quota system, such as teamwork, attending public service meetings, and eliminating public bias (Whisenand, 2011). If the public demands that police administration show productivity through quotas, then the officers will give the public what it demands, which are more tickets.

Some police departments use quotas as a way to collect and report numbers that are easy for the general public to understand. Quotas provide a mechanism to inform that public that the police are doing work. Indeed, if a police-community program was most effective and prevented all crime, then there would be no arrests. Therefore, in order to better serve the public by using crime preventative techniques, police administration must be willing to change its paradigm and implement a new method for assessing police officer performance (Whisenand, 2011).

In order to encourage police officers to serve the public, their performance reviews must reflect activities related to community policing. In other words, using quotas to gauge police performance will only promote egoism, which is self-serving. Thus, qualities such as problem solving, teamwork, initiative, judgment, commitment, and work quality must be assessed. See Table 5.

Table 5
Police Officer Public Service Performance Review (Whisenand, 2011)

CUSTOMER SERVICE (Problem Solving)	1	3	5
Participates in crime preventative programs (e.g., Neighborhood watch meetings)			
Positive community image			
Responsive to community requests			
Uses available community and government resources			
Follows up on services provided to residents			
TEAMWORK			
Displays behaviors that gain respect/trust from fellow officers			
Assists other officers			
Adequately resolves conflict			
Helps eliminate bias within the department			
Shares information that promotes police-community efforts			

COMMUNICATIONS			
Radio			
Reports			
Courtroom			
Listens to citizens			
Ability to adjust to audience			
INITIATIVE			
Identifies and addresses community concerns			
Requires minimal supervision			
Serves as a role model			
Strives to improve performance			
Follows up on work details on own initiative			
Productivity meets the expectations that were agreed upon			
JUDGEMENT			
Aware of consequences of work-related decisions			
Ability to make best-practice decisions with available information			
Sensitive to the needs of the community			
Use of discretion			
Willing to take reasonable risks			
WORK QUALITY			
Knows law			
Applies law			
Effectively uses available equipment			
Completed work product (e.g. reports, collecting evidence)			

PERSONAL APPEARANCE			
Uniform			
Police Car			
Driving			
COMMITMENT			
Pride in department			
Loyalty to department			
Helps eliminate conflict in the community			
OVERALL SCORE			
REMARKS TO IMPROVE PERFORMANCE			
INCREASE IN SALARY BASED ON PERFORMANCE SCORE: IF SCORE > 50% THEN INCREASE IN SALARY = [% SCORE] x [.07] CURRENT SALARY IF SCORE < 50% THEN DECREASE IN SALARY = [% SCORE] x [.07] CURRENT SALARY			

Below is an example of how a police chief can use quotas (descriptive statistics) to control the crime rate and to deceive other people.

The police chief approaches the board and asks for additional monies. The chief states that if additional monies are denied, then the crime rate will increase. Suppose the board denies additional monies. The chief will then tell his officers to file two charges for each person incarcerated (each charge is considered an arrest). Thus, the crime rate, which is based on the number of arrests, just doubled. The chief approaches the board and informs them of the 100% increase in crime. After the board approves the additional monies, the chief will then order his officers to file only one charge per person. Thus, the crime rate was cut by 50%.

As far as the community is concerned, the amount of criminal activity never changed.

Use the information below to make a decision.

City	2014 Reported Crime	2015 Reported Crime
A	100,000	100,000
B	100,000	200,000

After the 2015 results are published, you plan to move to either City A or City B.

Which city is safer?

Answer: Insufficient data to answer question.

1) City A is currently safer if everything else is equal and if the crime rate in City B has doubled.

2) City B is currently safer if City B hired more police officers, who have arrested more of the criminals. The streets are now safer.

3) City A = City B if the arrest rate was manipulated by one simple command. For example, the police chief in City B may have ordered officers to file two charges for each event in order to double the arrest rate (perhaps to show that the crime rate is high in order to receive funds). For example, for each DUI investigation, police officers may be told to file DUI per se and DUI faculties impaired (i.e., two arrests for one event). After funds are received, the police chief may revoke his directive in order to prove that greater funds mean fewer crimes. By doing this, the police chief is able to control the crime rate at will.

Common Sense and False Complaints

ALLEN (2011, July 11) stated that the Indiana State Police administration fails to use common sense. For example, ALLEN stated that the administration no longer provides backup weapons and cell phones to troopers. This is a safety concern. Another concern that involves trooper safety is the constant threat of being improperly disciplined. Troopers may hesitate to be assertive and they may fail to take control of a situation because they are afraid that the administration will punish them. Indeed, new troopers are told in the field that command will side with whoever calls the post first. Therefore, if a trooper knows that a complaint will be made, then that trooper will need to call the post right away and explain the situation. If the complainant calls the post first, then the trooper will fight an uphill battle.

By placing citizen complaints under the category of unbecoming an officer, which covers many things (e.g., appearance, tone of voice, gestures, comments), police administration needs no further evidence to find a trooper guilty. The end result is that troopers may second guess their actions during critical situations. The results may be fatal.

Education

The Indiana State Police does not encourage advanced education (Allen, 2011, July 11). Although the Indiana State Police did require a college education at one time for new employees, the department has since "dummied down" the department (Allen, p. 7). According to ALLEN, the Superintendent has stated that lowering the standards will not impact the quality of recruits and will allow minorities to better meet the minimum requirements. ALLEN stated that this is offensive and suggests that women and blacks lack the ability to achieve. The fact that the Indiana State Police did not deny these claims during ALLEN's internal investigation is an adoptive admission that the department is intentionally offensive to minorities (del Carmen, 2010; Klein, 1997; Whitesell, 2011, August 30).

Federal Funds

When working federal projects, (e.g. operating while intoxicated patrol), troopers are supposed to be paid for all of the hours that they work (Allen, 2011, July 11). However, ALLEN stated that troopers are given time off instead. When ALLEN asked about the money, he was told by a superior officer to back off. The fact that the Indiana State Police did not deny these claims during ALLEN's internal investigation is an adoptive admission that the department may be mishandling federal funds (del Carmen, 2010; Klein, 1997; Whitesell, 2011, August 30).

Indiana State Police Alliance

In a recent letter issued by the Indiana State Police Alliance (ISPA), a club that supposedly represents the interests of troopers, the club condemned the actions of troopers who lodged complaints against the Indiana State Police (Rader, 2011). The ISPA condemned the complaints because a) they reflected personal opinions, b) they tarnished the department's image, c) the complaints have already been investigated by the state, and d) only the ISPA has the right to file complaints on behalf of state employees. Furthermore, the ISPA stated that feeding off opinions that reflect negatively upon the department is a destructive process, that only members of the ISPA can attend their meetings, and that the Indiana State Police administration sends a representative to monitor the ISPA meetings.

The preceding argument appears to be heavily biased against troopers. First, administrators are responsible for leading a team of diverse employees, who have a variety of skills (Whisenand, 2011). Good leadership requires listening to employees and it has been estimated that about 85% of a leader's abilities involve the ability to understand and use the power of emotions. Human nature involves emotions and opinions, and they provide information that cannot be obtained elsewhere. Thus, when the ISPA stated that they condemn the opinions of troopers, they are basically stating that qualitative information is unimportant (Rader, 2011). However, qualitative information is the only way to investigate why problems exist, and, therefore, opinions should be sought. Indeed, quantitative studies are ineffective for this type of study (Creswell, 2009). In other words, the ISPA does not understand the value of qualitative information and this limits their effectiveness at being trooper representatives. In addition, profound dissatisfaction is the catalyst for change (Whisenand). Only a person who is deeply dissatisfied, has much energy, is willing is break old bonds, and who has the insight to address sensitive issues can motivate change. In short, instead of dismissing the complaints of disgruntled employees, the ISPA should seek them in order to understand truth from the troopers' perspective (Berg, 2007).

Second, the courts and legislatures have recognized that police officers have a Constitutional right to free speech (Peak et al., 2010). Although the Supreme Court has indicated in *Pickering v. Board of Education* that the State does have an interest in controlling certain aspects of speech, and a state may impose restrictions on its employees that it would not be able to impose on nonemployees, the restrictions, however, must be reasonable. In the *Muller v. Conlisk* ruling, the Court ruled that a police department cannot arbitrarily regulate a police officer's free speech, even if it is derogatory toward the police department. According to the Indiana State Police policy, troopers cannot exercise their right to free speech (Whitesell, 2011, August 30). This rule is not supported by the *Muller v. Conlisk* ruling and should be challenged by troopers in court.

Third, the ISPA stated that complaints made against the state were investigated by the state, but this is inherently suspect (Rader, 2011). The methodology of the investigation and the actual data should be made available to the public for review (Creswell, 2009). If the data are not made available for others to scrutinize, then the study has little credibility and it would not be seriously considered by the experts. The ISPA failed to provide the study and, consequently, the argument is valueless.

Fourth, the ISPA implied that it engages in unethical behavior. For example, only ISPA members are allowed to attend meetings, only the ISPA can file complaints on behalf of troopers, and the Indiana State Police administration sends a representative to monitor the meetings (Rader, 2011). This is problematic because the ISPA discriminates against troopers who are not members. In addition, troopers may not want to file a complaint against the department in front of Indiana State Police management. The process is unethical because anonymity is lost (Creswell, 2009). In fact, the practice actually implies that Indiana State Police management has corralled troopers into ISPA meetings in order to identify complainants.

Finally, the ISPA stressed that the Indiana State Police's integrity was important (Rader, 2011). However, the ISPA did not explain why the Indiana State Police destroyed personnel records, destroyed electronic records, and failed to honor a subpoena during a 2011 court case (*Davis v. Whitesell, 2011*). The ISPA did state that the governor is a strong supporter of the Indiana State Police department.

Critical Thinking

Critical thinking is the open-minded, dynamic, and reflective process of collecting, analyzing, evaluating, and applying information in order to make best-practice decisions (Aiken Technical College, 2011). In law enforcement, police officers employ critical thinking skills when they evaluate the totality of the circumstances in order to establish probable cause and make decisions. In other words, police officers make the best decisions possible based on the available information. If the available information changes, then police officers should reassess the data and, perhaps, change their position; failure to change their position when the new data indicate that the initial decision was wrong is poor police work. Furthermore, police officers must understand that all decisions rely on assumptions. This is true because humans have limited intelligence and do not know everything. Indeed, if humans knew everything in the universe, then there would never be the need for a trial.

Laws & Rules

There are some laws, rules, and sayings that will help explain why police officers should work hard to effectively serve the public. First, according to Davis's Dictum, community problems that go away by themselves come back by themselves (Dickson, 1980). Hence, before trust can be effectively established, the root causes of mistrust must be understood. Second, according to Wolf's Law, a police officer does not get a second chance to make a first impression. Thus, police officers should always put forth their best efforts. Third, Winston's Second Rule of Success states that a police department's greatest assets are the local residents, who provide valuable resources. Indeed, social peace depends on the assistance provided by residents. Fourth, according to the Woolsey-Swanson Rule of Problems, individuals would rather live with problems that they cannot solve than solutions they cannot understand. Therefore, officers need to effectively communicate with the public. One way to do this is for the police departments to represent the community members that they serve (e.g., same % sex and race). Finally, Vietinghoff's Precept indicates that the managers who control the police forms control the program, which impacts the police department culture. In short, officer performance reviews are dictated by upper management via forms. Thus, upper management can endorse the behaviors that promote good police-community relations by using forms that assess officer performance based on police-community efforts instead of using forms that assess officer performance based on quotas.

There are some laws, rules, and sayings that will explain why some police officers resist working hard to effectively serve the public. First, according to the Upward-Mobility Rule, police officers should not work so hard that they are irreplaceable (Dickson, 1980). If the officers cannot be replaced, then they will not be promoted. Second, according to Rutherford's Rule, the less the officers know, the less work they will have to do. By investigating the community's concerns, the police department may be creating a lot of work. Third, according to Vaughan's Rule of Corporate Life, the lower an officer is on the organizational chart, the more work that officer will have to do. Although police management may make a lot of promises to the community, it is the officers who will get stuck with all of the work. Fourth, according to Toomey's Rule, it is easy to make decisions on matters in which the officers have no vested interest. If the officers have high stakes in the community, they may not be able to make the tough decisions. Fifth, according to Weiner's Wisdom, indecision is the key component to flexibility. Thus, if a police-community program is implemented and it is less than optimal, the department may be too invested and too committed to change its position. Finally, according to Rigsbee's Principle of Management, the brightest and best employees will be the first officers to leave the department when given the opportunity. In other words, if officers demonstrate superior skills in serving the public, other departments may seek to hire them and, if the officers leave the department, the department will lose much money that was invested in the officers' training.

Recommendations for Indiana State Police Problem

There are several ways for the Indiana State Police department to improve its image, credibility, and performance. First, the department must change its culture, starting with the elimination of its long-standing age discrimination policy. This will show a sincere desire to change for the better. Second, officers must be persuaded to change their own behaviors. However, change must come from the top; without motivation to change, officers will continue to reflect upper management. Third, the department must hire educated individuals. The police cannot effectively serve the public if they do not understand the public. Fourth, the *Giglio* policy should be adopted by all police departments. Trust and credibility require that the police officers who are on duty tell the truth when they are required to be truthful. If the officers cannot be truthful when they are required to be truthful, then they should not have authority over other people's freedom. Fifth, the Indiana State Police should send their Quarterly Disciplinary reports to the media. If police management expects to get the respect and trust of the community, then management needs to be less secretive. Sixth, instead of using quotas, performance reviews should reflect activities that are related to community policing. Using creative ways to assess performance requires educated management. Finally, the police department should reflect the community that it serves (same % sex and race). To enhance communication, job effectiveness, justice, and public trust, the police department must reflect the local community. Reflecting the community will enhance the department's understanding of the community.

Table 6
Improving Police Image, Credibility, and Performance

7 Ways for the Indiana State Police Department to Improve its Image, Credibility, and Performance
Stop Practicing Age Discrimination
Officers must change their own behaviors
Hire educated officers
Giglio policy should be made into department policy
Department should send their Quarterly Disciplinary reports to the media
Performance reviews must reflect activities related to community policing
Department must reflect the community that it serves (same % sex and race)

References

Aiken Technical College (2011). *Achieve more with critical thinking.* Retrieved from http://www.atc.edu/p371.aspx

Allen, C. (2011, July 11). *The Indiana State Police facade.* Electronic letter mailed to Indiana state employees on July 11, 2011.

Berg, B.L. (2007). *Qualitative research methods for the social sciences* (6th ed.). Boston, MA: Pearson.

Creswell, J.W. (2009). *Research design: Qualitative, quantitative, and mixed methods approaches* (3rd ed.). Los Angeles, CA: Sage.

Davis v. Indiana State Police, 541 F.3d 760 (7th Cir. September 3, 2008).

Davis v. Whitesell, No. 10-2617 (7th Cir. July 5, 2011).

Del Carmen, R.V. (2010). *Criminal procedures: Laws & practice* (8th ed.). Belmont, CA: Wadsworth.

Dickson, P. (1980). *The official explanations.* New York, NY: Delacorte.

Getts, M. (2011, July 10). *Trooper resigned because of traffic policies.* KPCnews.com

Klein, I. (1997). *Law of evidence for criminal justice professionals* (4th ed.). Belmont, CA: Wadsworth.

Kraska, P. (2004). *Theorizing criminal justice: Eight essential orientations.* Long Grove, IL: Waveland Press, Inc.

LexisNexis (2008). *Indiana criminal and traffic law manual.* Charlottesville, VA: Matthew Bender.

Long, B., & Yerington, C. (2006). Police administrators in Indiana: A descriptive study of attitudes, perceptions, and stressors. *Internet Journal of Criminology,* 1-23.

Miller, M.R., Schultz, D.O., & Hunt, D.D. (2011). *Police patrol.* Mason, OH: Cengage.

Peak, K.J., Gaines, L.K., & Glensor, R.W. (2010). *Police supervision and management in an era of community policing* (3rd ed.). Upper Saddle River, NJ: Prentice Hall.

Rader, J. (2011, July 14). *Department morale.* Letter distributed by Indiana State Police Alliance.

U.S. Department of Homeland Security (2004). *Law course for customs and border protection officers.* Longwood, FL: Gould.

Whisenand, P.M. (2011). *Supervising police personnel: The fifteen responsibilities* (7th ed.). Upper Saddle River, NJ: Prentice Hall.

Whitesell, P. (2011, August 30). *Disciplinary actions – finding and order.* Indiana State Police, Indianapolis, IN.

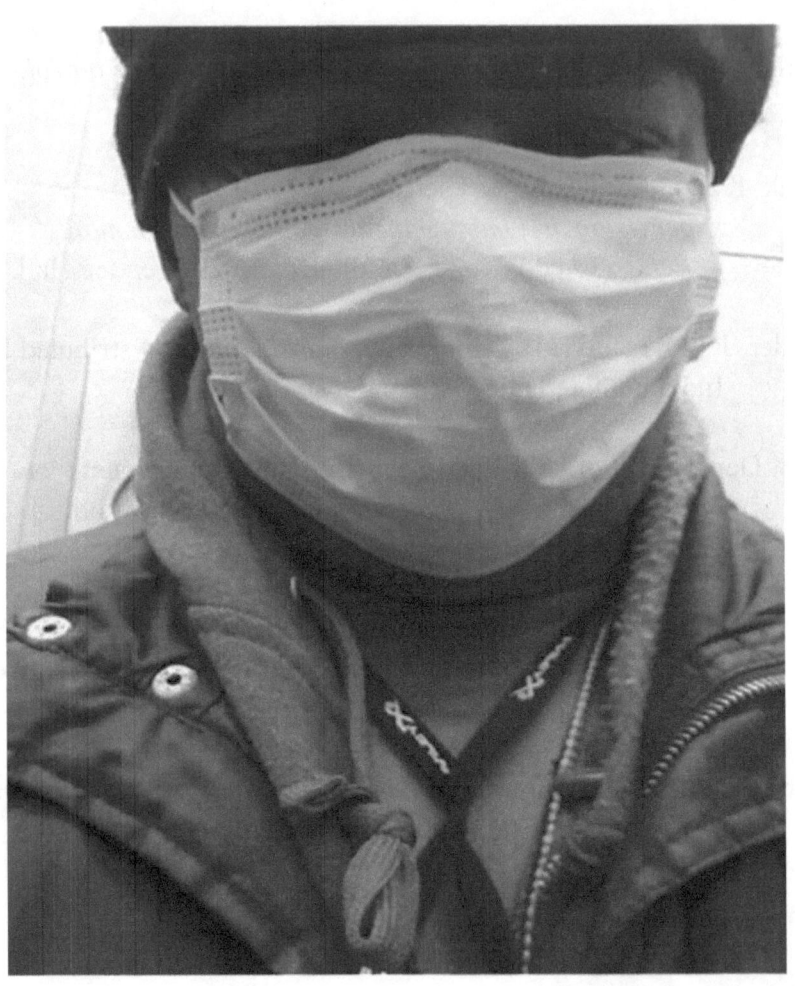

www.ingramcontent.com/pod-product-compliance
Lightning Source LLC
Chambersburg PA
CBHW020904310526
45786CB00018B/1771